Peak and
Pennine country

PEAK & PENNINE COUNTRY

W. A. Poucher

Constable   London

First published in Great Britain 1991
by Constable and Company Limited
3 The Lanchesters, 162 Fulham Palace Road
London W6 9ER
Copyright © 1991 pictures, The Estate of W. A. Poucher
Copyright © 1991 text, John Poucher
The right of W. A. Poucher and John Poucher to
be identified as the authors of this Work has been
asserted by them in accordance with the
Copyright, Designs and Patents Act 1988
ISBN 0 09 470560 7
Text filmset by BAS Printers Limited,
Over Wallop, Hampshire
Printed and bound in Spain by
Graficas Estella, S.A.

A CIP catalogue record for this book
is available from the British Library

The photographs

Preface

This book, containing a further one hundred of my father's superb pictures, is published as a companion volume to *The Yorkshire Dales and the Peak District* which appeared in 1984. The photographs in the two volumes depict the most interesting and most beautiful features of that wonderful wild region.

These photographs were taken over a period of years during my father's visits to the area which began around 1946, but today's readers will find that the pattern of the countryside remains essentially unchanged, although some of the man-made features which appear in the pictures may have vanished and new ones may have been added.

The photographs have been arranged in a roughly south-to-north progression up 'the backbone of England', from Derbyshire's delightful Dovedale to historic Hadrian's Wall in Northumberland, and though most of the subjects may be seen by the motorist as he or she drives northwards, in some cases – particularly those wonderfully scenic valleys of the Peak District – it is necessary to leave the car and tramp through the countryside on foot in order to appreciate to the full its beauty and charm.

As a boy, and later as an adult, I often accompanied my father on walks in the Lake District, Snowdonia and the Highlands of Scotland, but in the case of the Peak and Pennine country I have walked with him only in my imagination while viewing the slides he showed my wife and me. His commentary on his wanderings was so vivid that we followed him step by step – along the Derbyshire Dales, through the peat groughs on Kinder Scout and Bleaklow, over Derwent Edge with its collection of unusual obelisks, on to Ilkley Moor with its Cow and Calf Rocks, to Brimham, Wensleydale, and points north. Indeed, he fired us with such enthusiasm that we could not wait to visit the region for ourselves.

I hope that the beauty of the photographs contained in this book may similarly inspire all those who read it.

John Poucher
Gate Ghyll, High Brigham,
Cockermouth, Cumbria
1991

Dovedale

This is one of the loveliest dales in the Peak
District. A short walk from the car-park brings
you to these stepping stones set in the clear waters
of the River Dove. If you omitted to cross the
river by the wooden bridge lower down, and wish
to continue walking up the dale, you must try
crossing here – and if the river is high this may
prove quite a hazardous enterprise.

Ilam Rock
(overleaf)

Some $1\frac{1}{2}$ miles further up Dovedale this spectacular limestone pinnacle rears up on the far bank of the river like a gigantic tooth. The tors and needles with which the valley walls bristle have become a great attraction for rock climbers and several routes have been developed on Ilam Rock.

Pickering Tor
(overleaf p 15)

The path beyond Ilam Rock yields this view of the craggy tor, which you will already have passed on your walk up Dovedale. Like Ilam Rock, it is visited by the modern generation of rock climbers.

Tissington

This pretty village lying to the east of Dovedale
is noted for its picturesque well-dressing
ceremony which takes place every year on
Ascension Day.

Brassington Rocks

(overleaf)

These rocks, named Rainster Rocks on the OS map, are about a mile west of the tiny village of Brassington. Although they are only a small feature, they consist of dolomite, a form of limestone which is not often found in Britain, and so they are of interest to rock climbers.

Cromford Black Rocks

This striking and picturesque outcrop of gritstone
is a landmark just south of Cromford on the edge
of Cromford Moor. The rocks are not actually
black, as can be seen in the picture, but since they
face north the sunlight is always behind them, and
silhouetted against the sky they appear black and
forbidding.

The summit

This is one of the five huge bastions around the summit of the Black Rocks, each of a strange and dominating beauty. There is an easy path by which pedestrians can reach the top.

High Tor and Riber Castle

(overleaf)

The prominent limestone outcrop of High Tor near Matlock Bath rises commandingly over both the River Derwent and the busy A6. It provides steep and difficult climbing, often exposed to wild weather. The ruins of Riber Castle, built in 1850, rise imposingly against the sky to the north-east.

The Inaccessible Pinnacle

The remarkable gritstone outcrop known as Robin Hood's Stride is characterized by two fluted pinnacles some 30 feet apart – not an easy step from one to the other even for the legendary outlaw! The photograph shows the larger of the two pinnacles, to the west; the other, standing nearer Cratcliffe Tor, is known to climbers as The Weasel. Paths from every side lead to the platform between the pinnacles.

Lathkill Dale
(*overleaf*)

Soft autumn colours enhance the beauty of this much loved dale, whose narrowest and loveliest section, beyond Conksbury Bridge, is well wooded, with trees descending to the very edge of the river. The houses of Over Haddon can be seen in the distance.

The River Lathkill
(*overleaf pp 30/31*)

The Lathkill, which threads the dale, is one of the prettiest rivers in the Peak District, as it ripples over little weirs and cascades on its way to join the River Bradford, in the dappled shade of overhanging trees.

Haddon Hall

Standing beside the River Wye, this famous and
romantic twelfth- to fifteenth-century English
mansion, with a notable chapel and hall, lies some
two miles south-east of Bakewell. It is associated
with Dorothy Vernon and her romance with John
Manners, and it is open to the public on most
weekdays.

Ashford village

Storm clouds gather over this picturesque stone village, lying on the River Wye above Bakewell. Beyond it, Monsal Dale opens up to ramblers, who should choose to walk the western bank of the stream.

Miller's Dale

This well-wooded valley, blazing in autumn with russet and gold, carries the River Wye and lies between Chee Dale and Monsal Dale. The three dales as a whole are a paradise for the walker. Those who are photographers as well will find it best to walk up them rather than down, for the waterplay of the river is then seen to best advantage, and the sun illuminates Monsal and Chee Dales better in the morning.

Chee Dale
(*overleaf*)

When this picture was taken years ago, Chee Dale was the preserve of the rambler. Today its formidable overhanging buttresses, which are best photographed in afternoon light, are a great attraction for rock climbers, who have explored the cliffs throughout the dale.

The Goyt Valley
(*overleaf pp 40/41*)

In this narrow valley to the west of Buxton the stream is hemmed in by moorland slopes whose colourful tapestry appeals to both artist and photographer. The tumbling waters rise on Axe Edge Moor near the Cat and Fiddle Inn (see next picture). Those wishing to walk up the valley will do best to leave their cars at the Goytsclough Quarry.

Shining Tor

The gentle summit on the skyline is the usual
objective of those walking up Goyt Valley, but it
can more quickly be reached from the Cat and
Fiddle – a famous inn standing at the high point
of the Buxton-to-Macclesfield road.

Ramshaw Rocks

(overleaf)

Seen against the sky long before they are reached, these strange gritstone rocks are clustered thickly on a conspicuous rise, and come as a pleasant surprise after the bleak moors of Axe Edge. They are worth looking at closely, and yield an interesting panorama from their summit.

Hen Cloud from Upper Hulme

Rising sharply from the moor and the charming
hamlet of Upper Hulme, Hen Cloud is crowned
by a ring of symmetrical gritstone buttresses,
which combine with its pyramidal form to give
the appearance of a real mountain. It offers the
rock climber excellent sport.

On Hen Cloud

(*overleaf*)

From the summit of Hen Cloud a spectacular panorama of Staffordshire countryside unfolds. Bow Buttress forms the end of this ridge, with the Arête climb below it.

The Roaches

The prominent bastions of The Roaches are the most awe-inspiring gritstone outcrop in the Pennines. They are divided into two bands of rock, the Upper and Lower Tiers. Into the Lower Tier has been built the Gamekeeper's Cottage, embowered in trees.

Birchen Edge

(overleaf)

The eastern Edges of the Peak District extend
northwards along the Derwent valley for some
fifteen miles from Chatsworth. They are like the
long, broken battlements of some majestic fort,
and look their best in the light of the evening sun.

Apple Buttress

(overleaf p 53)

This fine buttress, rising up on Gardom's Edge
and overlooking the Bar Brook valley, has a name
with romantic associations. In the 1930s a man
cleaning the crack for climbing found a lovely
apple in it, which he ate. He later met the lady
who had left it there – and married her.

Bar Brook

(overleaf pp 54/55)

This stream flows down the valley between
Birchen and Gardom's Edges, with the moors
above Sheffield stretching away in the distance.

The Wellington Monument

Baslow Edge frowns upon Bar Brook in the valley below, and on a sunny afternoon opens up spacious views and a superb prospect of the whole of Gardom's Edge on the rim of the moor opposite. The southern extremity of Baslow Edge is crowned with the Wellington Monument.

The Great Buttress

(overleaf)

Curbar Edge lies above the village of the same name, and can be ascended by several tracks from the valley below. Prominent on the Edge is The Great Buttress, with its ferocious cracks and walls.

Stoney Middleton

(overleaf p 60)

This village in Middleton Dale lies to the west of Curbar Edge and is dominated on the north by a line of vertical limestone cliffs whose rock climbs are technically as difficult as any in Britain. The best view of these is from the crest of the ridge to the south of the dale.

Climbing on the cliffs

(overleaf p 61)

Clinging to the rock with toes and fingers, defying gravity, rock climbers inch their way up the formidable cliffs of Stoney Middleton. Great classic climbs from several generations co-exist here.

The *leaning pinnacle*

Froggatt Edge, about a mile long, is one of the finest of the eastern Edges, and rewards the walker with glorious views. Towards the north of the Edge is this strange projecting pinnacle.

Lawrencefield

Hidden from passing travellers, this abandoned quarry can be reached by a grassy path from the Surprise View on the A625. The Great Wall, with a dark and sinister pool lying at its base, is almost vertical and offers sheltered rock-climbing on chilly days.

Millstone Edge

(overleaf)

This conspicuous Edge was once an immense quarry and its sheer faces are seen to best advantage on a sunny afternoon. This is the Great Slab area, reached by an easy walk from the A625.

Burbage Brook

This stream ripples down the valley between
Burbage Rocks to the east and Carl Wark to the
west. By crossing this bridge and walking
through heather and boulders, you will reach the
less-frequented southern section of Burbage
Edge; tracks also lead from here to Carl Wark.

Burbage Rocks

Burbage Rocks, in a romantically isolated setting,
are two miles long and divided into a northern
and a southern section. This fine view is of part
of the southern section, on a clear day in autumn.

Carl Wark

Crowning the bold outcrop of gritstone like an
ancient fortification – which it once was – Carl
Wark slopes upward from west to east and
terminates in a sharp prow, supported on all sides
by shattered crags and boulders. Stones of the old
defence walls can still be seen there.

Higgar Tor
(overleaf)

This tremendous leaning tower characterizes Higgar Tor, an escarpment which tops this hill behind Millstone Edge. The Tor reaches the 1,400-foot contour and its magnificent views are a fitting climax to a walk which starts at Burbage Brook and scrambles over Carl Wark.

Stanage Edge

Stanage Edge, about four miles long, is the most
splendid of all the Edges. Where the high plateau
of Hallam Moor ends suddenly, a line of
precipitous gritstone cliffs, up to 100 feet high,
separates it from the valley, which sinks gently
down to woods fringing the river at its foot. On
a favourable afternoon the cliffs gleam like gold
in the westering sunlight.

The Cowper Stone

This landmark juts against the sky at the southern end of Stanage Edge. Above it begins a path that runs along the crest of the ridge for four miles, with superb views into the valley of the River Derwent.

Jacob's Ladder

This rock staircase, which climbs up one of the breaks in Stanage Edge, has been a pathway for travellers from ancient times. Known as Jacob's Ladder, it is part of the old Roman road which ran from the Redmires reservoirs via Long Causeway down towards Hathersage in the valley below.

Bamford Edge

This lofty escarpment yields an extensive
panorama that includes the Ladybower Reservoir,
just glimpsed in this picture. Bamford Edge is on
private land belonging to the Water Board, and
is characterized by a number of bold buttresses.

The Rivelin Needle

This dramatic and unusual gritstone pinnacle is a special feature of Rivelin Edge, which, for all its rocky and heathery terrain, in fact lies within Sheffield City boundaries. First conquered in 1932, the Needle still attracts swarms of rock climbers.

Ladybower Reservoir

(overleaf)

The clear waters of the Ladybower Reservoir mirror its surrounding hills on a fine day. Prominent just to the right of centre is Derwent Edge. The northern arm of this reservoir fills the southern end of Derwent Dale, and its western arm the Woodlands valley. The bridge in the photograph carries the A57 across the junction of its two arms.

Derwent Edge

Standing in splendid isolation on the very edge of
the moor, the Wheel Stones are the most
remarkable outcrop of rocks on Derwent Edge.
This, the most northerly of the Edges, offers the
finest walk in the Peak District, for though it has
no continuous line of cliffs it is high enough to
reveal a panorama that delights the eye from start
to finish.

White Tor

The prominent crags of White Tor rise against the
sky not far beyond the Wheel Stones, on the rim
of Derwent Edge.

The Salt Cellar

(overleaf)

This famous and extraordinary obelisk stands below the crest of Derwent Edge and may easily be missed by the unobservant walker. On a clear day it is a magnificent viewpoint for Howden Moor to the north and the desolate uplands of Kinder and Bleaklow.

Dovestones Tor

Many walkers stop at the Salt Cellar (previous photograph) but it is well worth while continuing along Derwent Edge to this outcrop of gritstone, which has a cave at its foot, and is comparatively seldom visited by rock climbers.

Cakes of Bread
(overleaf)

Cottage Loaves might possibly be a more appropriate name for these strange rocks, which lie along the walker's path before he or she reaches the end of Derwent Edge, at Back Tor.

The Winnats
(overleaf pp 98/99)

This narrow, sweeping and pinnacled ravine was formed aeons ago by the action of water on the soft limestone of the region. This resulted in a gigantic cavern whose roof collapsed when the waters subsided. Those with a steady head who wish to admire fully the splendour of this amazing gash in the landscape should walk along the crest of the cliffs and gaze across the valley at Win Hill in the far distance.

Mam Tor from Castleton

The 'Shivering Mountain', so called because of
the constant disintegration of its shaly face, forms
the distinctive western end of a ridge leading as
far as Lose Hill. For the sake of brevity my father
called this The Great Ridge. Mam Tor, whose
shattered face is the Ridge's most striking feature,
is seen to best advantage from the neighbourhood
of Castleton, as in this photograph.

The Great Ridge

(overleaf)

The Great Ridge is four miles long and the only ridge of its kind in the Peak District. Here, with Back Tor and Lose Hill in the distance, is Hollins Cross – the col where the path from Edale to Castleton crosses the Ridge.

Back Tor

(overleaf pp 104/105)

This is the most striking section of the walk along The Great Ridge, for the crumbling precipices of Back Tor contrast boldly with the smooth green slopes of the Ridge and the flat skyline of the distant Edges. If you walk the Ridge in an easterly direction this is the last rise you will meet before Lose Hill. The plantation on the south ridge is much depleted since my father's day.

The start of the Pennine Way

This first and most famous of Britain's long-
distance footpaths starts here, in the pretty village
of Edale, and runs northwards for some 250 miles
to Kirk Yetholm just over the Scottish border.
Countless thousands have set out along this path
since the Way was officially opened in 1965.

The River Noe

(overleaf)

An old packhorse bridge spans the River Noe in the upper reaches of Edale, and from here a steep track known also as Jacob's Ladder (see page 80 for another) forms the alternative start of the Pennine Way from Edale. This path, after passing Edale Cross and Kinderlow, joins the main track above Kinder Downfall.

Kinder Downfall

(overleaf p 109)

On the western edge of Kinder Scout the River Kinder normally plunges some 100 feet over these rocks and precipices. This picture, however, was taken in a very dry spell, and there is no trace of it. In severe winters huge icicles form here and hang gleaming from the cliffs.

Seal Edge

The circuit of the edges of Kinder Scout makes
a fine expedition for a hardy walker. Its 22 miles
of varied scenery and magnificent views can be
done in a day by the energetic. Seal Edge rises on
the northern rim of the plateau.

Pym's Chair

Eye-catching gritstone obelisks greet those
walking the circuit of the Kinder plateau. This
does not look a very comfortable seat!

Bleaklow

(overleaf)

The Pennine Way passes over this vast, lonely moorland uplift north of Kinder – a wilderness of grass, bog, and peat groughs, riven by streams and cloughs. Any walker here is well advised to take both a map and a compass. On the horizon in the picture rises Higher Shelf Stones (see next photograph).

Higher Shelf Stones

This is the most impressive section of the walk
across Bleaklow, and one of the few prominent
landmarks available to guide walkers there. The
fine elevation of the Higher Shelf Stones is seen
in this picture to advantage.

The approach to Laddow Rocks

The Pennine Way runs along the crest of Laddow
Rocks, the most northerly and isolated of the
better known gritstone outcrops in the Peak
District National Park. The popular approach to
them starts at Crowden, at the crossing of
Crowden Great Brook.

The Long Climb

Laddow Rocks was at one time the most popular climbing venue for Mancunians, and this is one of the many routes on its excellent cliff face. It is here that we leave the Peak District to travel north along the Pennines.

Rocky Valley

(overleaf)

The popular Yorkshire resort of Ilkley is a favourite haunt of rock climbers, for the lofty stretch of wild moorland has three separate groups of crags. This valley boasts six buttresses – this, No 6, is the finest.

Almscliff

This conspicuous gritstone outcrop crowns a
small hill about a mile north of the village of
Huby. It is divided into two separate tiers: this
upper one, called High Man, might almost be two
adjacent Dartmoor tors, as it is cleft by a narrow
break called the Rift.

Plumpton Rocks

(overleaf)

Most of these rocks are hidden in densely growing trees, but these, frowning over a lake, can clearly be seen across its green waters. Since they are on a private estate, a small fee is payable before you can visit them.

Brimham Rocks

Brimham Moor boasts an astonishing collection of pinnacles, tors and boulders, ample evidence of the powerful eroding qualities of wind, water and frost. This fantastic rock garden, which has become the playground of the rock climber, is owned by the National Trust.

In Stump Cross Caverns

(overleaf)

These privately owned underground caverns were first discovered in about 1860. A good path through them, and electric lighting, makes it possible to examine the astonishing stalactites at close quarters, and to marvel at their varied shapes and colours. The entrance to the caverns is on the moor to the south of the B6265, about six miles from Grassington.

Fountains Abbey

The graceful remains of this Cistercian abbey,
founded in 1132, lie beside the River Skell in the
park of Studley Royal. It is beautifully maintained
by the National Trust.

Bolton Abbey

(overleaf)

A perfect study of these exquisite twelfth-century
ruins, in the golden stillness of an autumn
afternoon. They stand in the lovely Yorkshire
valley of Wharfedale, whose lower reaches are
well explored on foot from this point.

Burnsall

The River Wharfe ripples through this charming
stone village, which nestles in its peaceful valley.

Kilnsey Crag

(overleaf)

This stupendous limestone escarpment rears its massive bulk to the left of the road that leads up Wharfedale. The famous overhang, which can be discerned on the left, is a major rock-climbing problem, and all the routes on this steep crag are for top-ranking climbers only.

Littondale

A by-road branches to the left of the road through
Wharfedale, some $2\frac{1}{2}$ miles south of Kettlewell,
and threads this quiet and pleasant valley which
carries the River Skirfare.

Starbotton

The cottages of this pretty village, standing on the
east bank of the River Wharfe, are tucked away
under the brow of Cam Head. It is a perfect place
to linger awhile as you explore the dale.

Cray Gill
(overleaf)

The delightful cascade of this tributary of the River Wharfe graces a small cove in upper Wharfedale. It can be found about a mile north of Buckden, not far from the B6160 which runs northwards over the high moors before descending through Bishopdale into Wensleydale.

Langstrothdale
(overleaf pp 146/147)

After leaving Buckden, take the left fork and you will enter this serene landscape where the infant Wharfe, babbling in its stony bed, is at its most picturesque.

Malham village

Standing athwart the River Aire, this village
makes a convenient base for visiting the
magnificent limestone outcrops nearby. It can be
reached by a narrow road which leaves the A65
in Coniston Cold.

Malham Cove

(overleaf)

This stupendous semicircle of limestone cliffs, about a mile north of Malham, is more than 300 feet high and is one of the scenic and geological wonders of the Pennines. A waterfall once plunged over the rim to the valley below, but Malham beck now emerges from the foot of the cliffs. Photographers should ideally visit Malham Cove on a sunny day, early in the afternoon, when the lighting will throw into superb relief every detail of the immense façade.

Gordale Scar

(overleaf p 152)

Many people think this spectacular limestone defile even more impressive than Malham Cove. The towering mural precipices are some 200 feet high and the topmost waterfall gushes from a window far up in the limestone face. The noise of the turbulent waters fills the whole narrow gorge, which William Wordsworth thought one of the grandest objects in nature.

Dry Valley

(overleaf p 153)

At the head of the valley pictured here a waterfall once cascaded down on the right, and the stream flowed on down the valley to dive over the rim of Malham Cove.

Malham Tarn

This blue sheet of water lies cradled on the moors
less than two miles north of the Cove, and Tarn
House is pleasantly situated above its north shore.
It was at Tarn House that Charles Kingsley wrote
part of *The Water Babies*.

Great Close Scar

The Craven Fault area is notable for its limestone
escarpments or scars, some rising to a height of
1,350 feet. This one can be seen on the eastern side
of Malham Tarn, while to the left in the
photograph there is a glimpse of Highclose Scar,
darkly outlined against the blue of the sky.

Attermire Scar

(*overleaf*)

Another of these lonely limestone scars, some two miles north-east of Settle, is Attermire, which contains a cave where remains of animals dating from the Great Interglacial period were discovered during the nineteenth century. The whole area is patterned with a maze of high stone walls that need careful negotiation.

Penyghent

The Pennine Way passes over the summit of this
attractive mountain, one of the trio known as
'The Three Peaks', the other two being
Whernside and Ingleborough. Penyghent is seen
here from the east, with the summit on the left
and Plover Hill to the right. The walk to its
summit is invigorating, and unfolds a spacious
prospect in all directions.

Trow Gill

Those ascending Ingleborough from the direction
of Clapham will pass through this impressive
limestone ravine, which centuries ago probably
carried off water from the eastern flank of
Ingleborough.

Ingleborough
(overleaf)

After passing through Trow Gill (previous photograph) the path to Ingleborough emerges through a narrow gap on to the open moor. Those heading for the summit will cross the stone wall by the stile pictured here.

Simon Fell from Ingleborough

Ingleborough is one of the great landmarks of the Pennines, and dominates the vast moorland landscape from which it rises. Having reached its summit, you will be rewarded with this sweeping view of Simon Fell to the north-east.

Ribblehead Viaduct
(overleaf)

This fine viaduct at the head of Ribblesdale took some six years to complete and carries the Settle-to-Carlisle railway. The line runs northwards into the distance, threading many gloomy tunnels and passing over more viaducts in magnificent and wild high country on its way to the softer landscape of the Eden valley.

The River Dee in upper Dentdale

The water-music of the dales is one of the joys of
walking there – whether of large cataracts or, as
in this photograph, of the little cascades that grace
many streams and rivers. This peaceful spot is on
the left of the road that descends into lonely
Dentdale.

Dent station

This station, at an elevation of 1,145 feet, is the highest on any English main railway line. It was built as close to Dent village as was practicable, but is still more than four miles away!

Memorial stone

While wandering through the charming and
secluded village of Dent you will see this stone,
carved out of Shap granite, which commemorates
Adam Sedgwick, professor of geology and
Dentdale's most famous son.

Barbondale

(*overleaf*)

The road from Dent towards Kirkby Lonsdale
threads this quiet valley, where in the autumn the
bracken that clothes the hills so abundantly is cut
and stacked to be used as winter bedding for farm
animals.

Butter Tubs Pass

This lonely moorland road is the connecting link between upper Wensleydale and Swaledale to the north. The quaintly named 'Butter Tubs' are infant potholes with unusually fluted sides, grouped together to the left of the road as you travel north.

Gayle
(overleaf)

The stone cottages of Gayle, near Hawes, towards
the head of Wensleydale, stand on the edge of
Duerley Beck, which tumbles over broad ledges
through the centre of the village. In fine summer
weather they are a favourite playground for
children.

The Rawthey valley
(overleaf pp 182/183)

Beyond Sedbergh the road runs through this
beautiful valley on the way to Kirkby Stephen. It
is hemmed in by the Howgill Fells on one side and
by Baugh Fell on the other.

The Howgill Fells from the motorway

The rounded and imposing outlines of these
lonely hills rear up against the sky and form a fine
backdrop to the M6 between junctions 37 and 38.

Caldron Snout

The River Tees, the boundary between Yorkshire and Durham county, forms a series of spectacular cataracts where it foams over a bed of hard black basalt amid some of the wildest country in the Pennines. It is easy to scramble up the rocks on its eastern side and view the Snout in all its grandeur.

Cow Green Reservoir

This reservoir, which holds the waters of the
River Tees, lies above Caldron Snout (previous
photograph) and feeds its turbulent cascades. The
construction of the reservoir caused consternation
among naturalists, who feared the rare flora of
upper Teesdale would be destroyed.

High Cup Nick
(overleaf)

This gigantic gash in the earth may be reached by walking from Dufton, which is some four miles to the west. If you keep to the edge of its precipices until you reach its head, you can observe its peculiar formation – and on a clear day you can then see the far fells of Lakeland.

The Cross Fell range
(overleaf pp 192/193)

Cross Fell at 2,930 feet is the highest point in the whole Pennine range, and now lies just inside the Cumbrian border. It is really the culminating point of a lofty moorland plateau, and on most sides it is flanked by tracts of boggy moor which the rambler would do well to avoid. It is also often shrouded in low cloud.

Alston

This small, stone-built Cumbrian town is reputed
to be the highest market town in England. It is
a good place for those tramping the Pennine Way
to find accommodation and supplies.

Crag Lough

This shallow little lake lies right at the base of
High Shield Crag, and black basalt cliffs rise sheer
from its waters to a height of 200 feet. In the
distance Hadrian's Wall can be seen curving up
over Hotbank Crags.

Hadrian's Wall

(overleaf)

A superb study of this ancient fortification – the largest and most famous monument to the Romans in Britain, begun in AD 122 by the Emperor Hadrian. It runs up hill and down dale for 73 miles, from Bowness-on-Solway to Wallsend-on-Tyne, through magnificent and lonely countryside.

Housesteads North Gate

(overleaf pp 200/201)

Housesteads is the finest and best preserved of the seventeen forts that lie along Hadrian's Wall. Among its ruins have been discovered many interesting relics of equipment and possessions belonging to the Roman soldiers encamped there centuries ago.